FAVOURITE
YORKSHIRE
RECIPES

compiled by
Amanda Persey

with illustrations
by A.R. Quinton

SALMON

Index

Cover pictures *front:* "Whitby from East Cliff"
back: "White Wells, Ilkley Moor"
Title page: "Bootham Bar and the Minster, York"

Printed and Published by J. Salmon Ltd., Sevenoaks, England © Copyright

Yorkshire Pudding

4 oz. flour	**½ pint milk and water mixed**
¼ teaspoon salt	**2 tablespoons beef dripping**
2 medium eggs	**from the roasting tin**

Prepare the batter by placing the flour and salt into a large bowl. Make a well in the centre and break the eggs into this. Using a wooden spoon or an electric whisk, beat the eggs and gradually add the milk and water, incorporating the flour a little at a time. Beat until the batter is smooth and leave to stand in a cool place for about one hour. Remove the roast beef from the oven and keep warm or transfer to a lower shelf. Raise the oven temperature to 425°F or Mark 7. Place the beef dripping into a roasting tin 11 inch x 7 inch and place in the oven until very hot, by which time the oven will have reached the higher temperature. Remove from the oven and pour the batter into the tin. Return to a high shelf in the oven and cook for approximately 25 minutes until risen, golden brown and crisp. Cut into squares and serve immediately.

Yorkshire pudding was traditionally served before the roast beef to take the edge off the appetite and make the meat go further. Today it is often served as an accompaniment to the meat. It should be light, crisp and just slightly soft in the middle and is at its best straight from the oven.

Yorkshire Tea Cakes

½ oz. fresh yeast	2 oz. butter
½ pint tepid milk	1 oz. caster sugar
1 lb. strong white flour	4 oz. currants
1 level teaspoon salt	2 oz. chopped mixed peel

Milk to glaze

Heat oven to 400°F or Mark 6. Blend the yeast with a little of the tepid milk to form a creamy liquid. Place the flour and salt into a large bowl and rub in the butter. Stir in the sugar, currants and mixed peel. Make a well in the centre and add firstly the yeast cream and then sufficient of the tepid milk to make a soft but not sticky dough. Turn on to a floured surface and knead until the dough is elastic. Cover with a damp cloth and leave to rise in a warm place until double in size. Divide into eight equal pieces and knead lightly into rounds 6 inches in diameter. Place on two baking trays and brush with milk. Cover with a cloth and prove in a warm place until double in size. Bake for 20 minutes until pale golden brown. Cool on a wire rack. Serve toasted with plenty of butter.

Barnsley Chops with Redcurrant Sauce

2 lamb loin chops per person, cut from the centre of the loin across both chops thus ending up with a butterfly shape   Oil for brushing

REDCURRANT SAUCE
4 tablespoons redcurrant jelly   1 wine glass port

Prepare the sauce by melting the jelly in a small pan. Add the port and bring to the boil. Boil for 5 minutes, reduce the heat and keep warm to serve with the lamb. Cook the lamb by brushing the chops with oil and grilling for 8–9 minutes turning occasionally. The chops should be well browned on the outside and slightly pink inside. Serve hot with the sauce.

Sticky Parkin

8 oz. flour	6 oz. black treacle
2 level teaspoons baking powder	4 oz. margarine
2 level teaspoons ground ginger	6 oz. soft brown sugar
1 level teaspoon ground cinnamon	1 egg, beaten
8 oz. medium oatmeal	¼ pint milk

Heat oven to 350°F or Mark 4. Grease and line with greaseproof paper the base and sides of a 9 inch square cake tin. Sieve the flour, baking powder, ginger and cinnamon into a large bowl and stir in the oatmeal. Put the treacle, margarine and soft brown sugar into a pan over a low heat and stir occasionally until the margarine has just melted. Make a well in the centre of the dry ingredients and gradually add the treacle mixture and then the egg and milk. Beat well until smooth. Pour into the tin and place in the oven for approximately one hour. Cool slightly in the tin and then turn onto a wire rack. Store in an airtight tin. Serve on its own or with butter.

Sticky Parkin is best kept in a tin for about a week before eating to allow it to become really moist; hence the name 'sticky'.

Yorkshire Baked Cheesecake

9 oz. shortcrust pastry

FILLING

2 oz. butter   **2 oz. caster sugar**   **12 oz. cottage cheese, sieved**
2 medium eggs, beaten   **3 oz. raisins**   **Grated rind and juice of one lemon**
2 oz. ground almonds

Roll out the pastry and line an 8 inch loose bottomed or spring-form deep flan ring. Chill in the refrigerator. Heat the oven to 375°F or Mark 5. Make the filling by creaming together the butter and sugar and gradually adding the cheese. Stir in the remaining ingredients and mix thoroughly. Spoon this into the pastry case, stand on a baking tray and cook in the oven for approximately 40 minutes until the filling is just set. If possible remove the sides from the flan ring and return to the oven for 10 minutes to ensure that the pastry sides are well cooked. Leave to cool and serve cold.

Bolton Abbey from Hartington Seat

Oat Cakes

8 oz. fine oatmeal   **Pinch bicarbonate of soda**
½ level teaspoon salt   **1 oz. butter**
Cold water to mix

Set oven to 300°F or Mark 2. Place the oatmeal, salt and bicarbonate of soda into a bowl. Rub the butter into the dry ingredients and add enough cold water to mix to a firm dough. Knead lightly on a surface dusted with oatmeal until the dough is smooth. Roll thinly and cut into round biscuits with a plain cutter. Place on a greased baking sheet and cook in the oven for 1 hour until crisp. Place on a wire rack to cool. Serve cold with butter and cheese.

Oat cakes are the perfect accompaniment to Wensleydale cheese.

Pickering Double Crust Pie

PASTRY
12 oz. flour   3 oz. butter   3 oz. lard   1 tablespoon caster sugar
1 egg yolk   Cold water to mix

FRUIT FILLING
1½ lbs. mixed soft fruits; blackcurrants, raspberries, gooseberries, etc.
4 oz. sugar, to taste

Put fruit in a heavy pan with sugar and bring to the boil; simmer gently until just soft. Leave to cool. Put flour into a large bowl and add butter and lard cut into small pieces. Rub the fat into flour until mixture resembles breadcrumbs. Stir in sugar with a blunt knife mix in egg yolk and sufficient cold water to make a binding dough. Chill in refrigerator for 20 minutes. Set oven to 400°F or Mark 6. Roll out half pastry and line a deep 8 inch pie dish. Strain fruit and reserve juice. Place the fruit in dish; roll out the remaining pastry to form lid. Damp edges of pastry with water and press well together. Use blunt knife to knock the edges together and flute. Bake for 40–50 minutes. Cover with foil if the pastry starts to over-brown; it is necessary to ensure that the pastry underneath fruit is cooked. Serve warm or cold with the fruit juice.

Scarborough Fish Cobbler

1½ lbs. cod or haddock   1 pint milk   1 bay leaf   2 oz. butter
2 oz. flour   1 onion, skinned and diced   4 oz. peeled prawns
1 tablespoon chopped fresh parsley   Juice of ½ lemon   Salt and pepper

SCONE TOPPING
8 oz. self-raising flour   Pinch salt   1 level teaspoon baking powder
1 level teaspoon dry mustard powder   2 oz. butter   3 oz. Wensleydale cheese, grated
1 egg   Nearly ¼ pint milk

Set oven to 425°F or Mark 7. Cook fish in a pan with half the milk with bay leaf; do not overcook. Reserve the liquid; skin and flake the fish. Melt butter in a pan, stir in flour and cook without browning, stirring all the time for 2 to 3 minutes. Remove from heat; stir in fish liquid and remaining milk. Return to heat and, stirring, bring to boil. When sauce thickens add onion and cook gently for 5 minutes. Remove from heat and add fish, prawns, parsley and lemon juice; season. Put into a 2½ pint ovenproof dish. Scone topping: place dry ingredients, except cheese, in a bowl. Rub in butter, stir in cheese, add egg and sufficient milk to make soft dough. Knead lightly, roll out to ½ inch thick and cut into small scones; arrange, overlapping around edge of fish mixture. Bake for 10 to 15 minutes until the scones are risen and golden brown.

South Bay, Scarborough

York Chocolate Pudding

6 oz. plain block chocolate   **A knob of butter**
3 tablespoons black coffee   **1 dessertspoon rum**
3 medium eggs, separated

Break the chocolate into pieces and place in a bowl standing over a pan of hot water. Add the coffee and stir until the chocolate has melted and is quite hot. Remove from the heat and stir in the butter and the rum. Add the egg yolks one at a time and stir well. Whisk the egg whites until they form soft peaks and fold into the chocolate mixture. Divide equally between six small dishes and cool in the refrigerator.

This is a very rich type of mousse.

Bean and Bacon Hotpot

1 lb. belly pork   2 cloves garlic, peeled and crushed
12 oz. piece of smoked bacon, cooked   2 x 15 oz. tins chopped tomatoes
1 tablespoon oil   1 level teaspoon dried mixed herbs   2 large onions, skinned and sliced
1½ lb. mixed cooked beans: red kidney beans, butter beans, etc.

Grill the belly pork, remove the rind and cut into ½ inch strip pieces. Cut the bacon into similar sized pieces. Set oven to 350°F or Mark 4. Heat the oil in a large frying pan and cook the onions until soft and transparent. Stir in the garlic, tinned tomatoes and herbs. Put a layer of the tomato mixture into a large deep casserole and cover with a layer of meat, followed by a layer of beans. Repeat until all the ingredients have been used up. Cover and cook for 1½ to 2 hours. Serve hot with crusty bread accompanied by a green salad.

Treacle Toffee

1 lb. soft brown sugar	**1 teaspoon malt vinegar**
¼ pint water	**6 oz. black treacle**
4 oz. butter	**2 oz. golden syrup**

Oil a shallow, 7 inch square tin. Place the sugar and water into a large saucepan over a low heat and allow the sugar to dissolve. Add the remaining ingredients and bring to the boil. Insert a sugar thermometer and boil without stirring until the mixture reaches 270°F 'soft crack' stage. If you do not possess a thermometer the toffee can be tested by dropping some mixture into cold water; when 'soft crack' stage is reached the syrup forms hard threads. Pour into the tin, allow to cool a little, mark into squares and leave to cool and set.

It is important when making toffee to use a large, heavy based saucepan, to prevent burning and boiling over.

Summer Pea Soup

2 oz. butter
1 lb. shelled peas
4 oz. spring onions
½ lettuce, washed and sliced

1 pint vegetable or chicken stock
4–6 mint leaves
Salt and freshly ground black pepper
1 level teaspoon sugar

Melt the butter in a large saucepan and add the peas, spring onions and lettuce. Cover and cook gently for 10 minutes, being careful not to brown the vegetables. Add the stock, mint, salt, pepper and sugar and cook until the peas are tender. Sieve or liquidize the soup until quite smooth. This soup is delicious served either hot or chilled, perhaps with a little cream and a few chives.

Apple and Oat Betty

3 oz. flour   3 oz. fine rolled oats   1 teaspoon ground cinnamon
½ teaspoon mixed spice   4 oz. butter   3 oz. demerara sugar
2 large cooking apples, peeled, cored and sliced   Rind and juice of one lemon
2 tablespoons orange marmalade

Set oven to 375°F or Mark 5. Put the flour, oats and spices into a large bowl. Add 3 oz. butter and cut into pieces with a knife and then rub into the dry ingredients until the mixture resembles breadcrumbs. Stir in the sugar. Toss the prepared apples in the lemon juice, rind and marmalade. Grease a 1½–2 pint ovenproof dish. Put half the apples in the dish and sprinkle half the oat mixture over them. Top this with the remaining apples and finally the rest of the oat mixture. Dot the top with the remaining 1oz butter. Cook for 45 minutes to 1 hour until the apples are tender and topping crispy. Serve warm.

Toad-in-the-Hole with Onion Gravy

**1 lb. pork sausages   4 tablespoons beef dripping   2 medium onions, skinned and sliced
1 tablespoon flour   ½–¾ pint beef stock**

BATTER
4 oz. flour   ½ level teaspoon salt   1 egg   ¼ pint milk   ¼ pint water

Batter: Put the flour and salt into a large bowl, make a well and add the egg. Whisk, gradually adding milk and water and drawing in the flour. Beat until smooth. Leave batter to stand for at least 30 minutes. Set oven to 425°F or Mark 7. Put half the dripping into a small roasting pan and place in oven until hot. Place sausages in the hot fat and return to oven for further 5 minutes. Pour batter over the sausages and cook for 40 minutes until well risen and golden brown. While Toad-in-the-Hole is cooking prepare the gravy. Put remaining dripping into a saucepan, add onions and cook gently until soft. Stir in the flour and cook until lightly browned. Remove from heat and gradually add beef stock, stirring well. Return to heat and bring to the boil. Simmer for 10 minutes and serve hot with the Toad-in-the-Hole.

North Country Apple Pie

15 oz. shortcrust pastry

FILLING
3 large cooking apples, peeled, cored and sliced   2 tablespoons water
2–4 oz. granulated sugar, depending on sweetness of apples
4 oz. Wensleydale cheese, thinly sliced   1 dessertspoon caster sugar

Prepare the apples and place in a large pan with the sugar and water. Cook until just soft. Strain the apples and reserve the juice to serve with the pie. Cool the apples. Set oven to 400°F or Mark 6. Divide the pastry in two and use one half to line a 9 inch pie dish. Place half the apples over the pastry and cover with a layer of Wensleydale cheese followed by the remaining apples. Roll out the rest of the pastry and use to cover the pie. Seal the edges by knocking the two layers of pastry together with a blunt knife, trimming and then fluting. Bake for approximately 35 minutes until pale golden brown. As soon as the pie is removed from the oven sprinkle with caster sugar. Serve warm with cream or custard.

Rhubarb Chutney

4 lb. rhubarb, trimmed and cut into small pieces	1 lb. raisins
1 lb. onions, skinned and diced	2 level teaspoons ground ginger
2 lb. demerara sugar	2 level teaspoons curry powder

1½ pints malt vinegar

Place the rhubarb, onions, sugar, raisins, spices and ½ pint of the vinegar in a large, thick-based saucepan and cook gently until the rhubarb is soft and tender. Add the rest of the vinegar and continue cooking steadily, stirring occasionally until of a thick consistency. Pot into clean, warm jars and cover.

This is an excellent way to use up the glut of rhubarb which most home growers experience.

Yorkshire Pork Pie

1lb. hot water crust pastry

FILLING
1½ lb. pork shoulder meat   8 oz. lean streaky bacon   1 level teaspoon salt
Freshly ground black pepper   1 teaspoon dry English mustard powder
1 level teaspoon dried sage   Beaten egg to glaze

Set oven to 425°F or Mark 7. Prepare the pastry. It is important to work hot water crust pastry while it is still warm. Cut off one quarter and leave covered; use rest to line a 6 inch loose-bottomed cake tin. Mould with fingers until it is about ½ inch from top of the tin. To prepare filling, mince or cut up finely the pork and bacon and then mix all ingredients together. Pack the meat mixture into the pastry case. Roll out remaining pastry into a circle and using a little beaten egg attach to the top of the pie. Decorate using the trimmings. Make ½ inch hole in the centre for steam to escape. Glaze with beaten egg. Bake for 15 minutes then reduce heat to 350°F or Mark 4 and bake for further 45 minutes. Remove from the tin. Brush sides with beaten egg and return to oven for 30 minutes until sides are golden. Serve warm or cold.

A.R.QUIN

Hot Red Cabbage

1½ lbs. red cabbage, finely shredded   2 oz. butter
2 large cooking apples, peeled, cored and sliced   ¼ pint cider vinegar
4 oz. redcurrant jelly

Melt the butter in a very large pan and add the apples and cabbage. Cover and sauté for 10 minutes, stirring occasionally. Add the vinegar, cover and cook very gently for 45 minutes to one hour, until the cabbage is just soft, stirring occasionally. Add the redcurrant jelly and mix in thoroughly. Cook for a further 15 minutes. This vegetable is delicious served hot with roasts and casseroles.

Millers Marmalade Pudding

3 tablespoons orange marmalade   4 oz. self-raising flour   4 oz. caster sugar
4 oz. soft margarine   1 level teaspoon baking powder   2 medium eggs   Grated rind one orange

SAUCE
4 tablespoons orange marmalade   ¼ pint water/orange juice mixed
2 level teaspoons arrowroot   2 tablespoons cold water

Grease a 2 pint heatproof pudding basin and place 3 tablespoons marmalade in the base. Put the flour, sugar, margarine, baking powder, eggs and orange rind into a large bowl, mix and beat well for 2–3 minutes until soft and of a smooth consistency. Alternatively use a food processor and mix for 30 seconds. Put this sponge mixture on top of the marmalade in the basin. Cover with a circle of greaseproof paper and then seal with foil. Cover and steam for 2 hours. Prepare the sauce by warming together in a saucepan the marmalade and water/orange juice mixture and simmer for 5 minutes. Blend the arrowroot and cold water to a smooth cream and stir in some of the marmalade mix. Return to the pan and heat, stirring until the sauce thickens and clears. Turn out the pudding onto a warm plate and serve hot with the sauce.

Beery Beef with Crusty Topping

1½ lbs. lean braising beef   2 slices back bacon, chopped   2 tablespoons oil
1 oz. butter   2 tablespoons flour   ½ pint bitter beer   ½ pint beef stock
1 teaspoon caster sugar   2 cloves garlic, peeled and crushed
2 medium onions, skinned and thinly sliced   2 carrots, peeled and sliced
1 bouquet garni   Salt and freshly ground black pepper

TOPPING
6 thick slices of white bread, buttered and spread with 1–2 tablespoons of grainy mustard
3 oz. Cheddar cheese, grated

Set oven to 325°F or Mark 3. Heat the oil and butter together in a frying pan, cut the meat into 1 inch cubes and fry a little at a time until well browned; place in a large casserole dish. Fry the bacon and transfer to the dish. Add the flour to the fat and cook, stirring until lightly browned. Gradually add the beer and stock and stir until the sauce thickens. Add one teaspoon of sugar. Put the garlic, onions and carrots in the casserole dish with the meat and pour the sauce over. Put in the bouquet garni and season with salt and pepper. Cook for 2½ hours until the meat is tender. The casserole will benefit by being stirred half way through cooking. Remove the bouquet garni and arrange the bread on top of the meat. Sprinkle the cheese over and grill until the cheese bubbles.

Cheese and Onion Bread

1 medium onion, skinned and diced	1 level teaspoon dry mustard
1 oz. butter	6 oz. Cheddar cheese, grated
1 lb. strong white flour	½ oz. fresh yeast
1 level teaspoon salt	½ pint tepid water

Set oven to 375°F or Mark 5. Cook the onion in butter until soft and transparent. Put the flour, salt, mustard and three-quarters of the cheese into a large bowl. Add a little of the tepid water to the yeast to make a smooth cream. Make a well in the dry ingredients and add yeast liquid, onions and enough of remaining water to make a soft, but not sticky dough. Turn on to a floured surface and knead well until dough is elastic. Cover with a damp cloth and leave to rise in a warm place until double in size. Knead again and divide in two. Place in two greased 1 lb. loaf tins. Leave in a warm place until dough reaches top of the tins. Sprinkle with remaining cheese and cook for 35–45 minutes until golden brown and shrunk slightly from sides of the tin. Turn out to cool on a wire rack. Serve warm with soup.

Granny Elsie's Tipsy Trifle

One 8 inch homemade sponge cake   2 oz. ratafia biscuits   8 oz. raspberry jam
1 wine glass sherry   8–12 oz. fresh raspberries, sprinkled with 1 oz. caster sugar

CUSTARD
½ pint milk   ½ pint single cream   4 egg yolks   2 level tablespoons caster sugar
1 teaspoon cornflour   2–3 drops vanilla essence

TOPPING
½ pint double cream   Lightly toasted flaked almonds

Spread the cake with the jam and cut into pieces. Place in the base of a wide, deep serving dish. Distribute the ratafia biscuits over the surface and sprinkle with sherry. Put the raspberries over this and leave to soak. Make the custard by heating the milk and single cream in a saucepan until hot but not boiling. Beat together the egg yolks, caster sugar, cornflour and vanilla essence and onto this pour a little of the hot milk/cream. Return this mixture to the pan and stir continuously over a gentle heat until the custard thickens. It will coat the back of a wooden spoon when ready. Do not overheat or the mix will curdle. Cool slightly and pour over the sponge and fruit base. When set, top with lightly whipped double cream. Decorate with the flaked almonds.

Thirty-One

Drop Scones

8 oz. self-raising flour   **1 level tablespoon caster sugar**
½ teaspoon salt   **1 large egg**
½ pint milk

Place the flour, salt and sugar into a bowl. Make a well in the centre and add the egg and the milk gradually, stirring to make a smooth, thick batter. Drop the mixture in tablespoons on to a hot, lightly greased griddle or heavy based frying pan. Keep the griddle at a steady, moderate heat and after 2–3 minutes when bubbles show on the surface of the scones, turn over and cook for 2 more minutes. Place the finished scones in a warm, folded tea towel; this will keep them warm and by keeping in the steam will prevent them from drying out. Serve warm with butter and jam or honey.

An excellent treat to make for the unexpected visitor as they are quick and made from store cupboard ingredients

A moorland road, Goathland

Swede and Apple Bake

**4 oz. butter   1 onion, peeled and diced   1 lb. swede, peeled and sliced into
¼ inch slices   2 medium cooking apples, peeled, cored and sliced
Salt and freshly ground black pepper
2 oz. fresh breadcrumbs, mixed with 2 oz. grated cheese**

Set oven to 375°F or Mark 5. Melt 2 oz. of the butter in a saucepan and cook the onion gently until soft. Arrange the onion, swede and apples in layers in a greased ovenproof dish, season between each layer and dot with the remaining 2 oz. butter. Top with the breadcrumbs and cheese mixture. Cover with kitchen foil and bake for 1 hour. Remove the cover and continue to cook until the topping is crisp and golden. Serve hot as a delicious accompaniment to pork or as a supper dish with crusty bread.

Crispy Crab Cakes from Whitby

8 oz. mixed prepared crab meat
2 oz. fresh white breadcrumbs
1 small egg, beaten
1 teaspoon Worcestershire sauce

½ teaspoon dry English mustard
2 spring onions, finely chopped
1 tablespoon lemon juice
Grated rind of one lemon

Oil for frying

Combine all the ingredients in a large bowl until well mixed. Divide the mixture into eight little cakes shaped roughly with floured hands and place on a baking tray. Chill in the refrigerator for 2–3 hours. Heat 2 tablespoons of oil in a shallow frying pan and, using a fish slice, place the cakes in the oil. Cook for 3 minutes on each side until golden brown. Drain on kitchen paper and serve immediately with lemon wedges.

Spiced Curd Tarts

12 oz. shortcrust pastry

FILLING
2 oz. butter   2 oz. caster sugar   1 medium egg   1 oz. self-raising flour
½ teaspoon ground cinnamon   ½ teaspoon ground mixed spice
Grated rind half a lemon   8 oz. curd cheese   3 oz. seedless raisins   3 tablespoons milk

Set oven to 350°F or Mark 4. Roll out the pastry to approximately ⅛ inch thick on a floured surface, cut into rounds with a large cutter and use to line 16 to 18 holes in bun trays. In a large bowl beat together the butter and sugar until pale and fluffy. Gradually mix in the egg and flour and then all the other ingredients. Divide this mixture evenly between the pastry cases and bake for approximately 30 minutes until the filling is golden in colour and set. Cool on a wire rack.

Brown Bread Cream with Damson Sauce

3 oz. stale wholemeal breadcrumbs   2 oz. caster sugar   ¾ pint milk
3 egg yolks   1 teaspoon cornflour   ½ oz. gelatine   4 tablespoons water
Juice of half a lemon   ¼ pint whipping cream

SAUCE
½ –¾ lb. damsons   ½ pint water   4 oz. granulated sugar

Place breadcrumbs and 1 oz. caster sugar on a baking tray and dry in moderate oven until evenly browned. Heat milk to near boiling. Beat together egg yolks, remaining caster sugar and cornflour and pour on some of the hot milk. Return to milk pan and stir continually until mixture thickens; do not boil. Soak gelatine in the water and lemon juice for few minutes. Strain the warm custard into a bowl and add soaked gelatine; stir until dissolved. Leave in a cool place; stir occasionally. When custard is cold, whip the cream to floppy consistency and fold in. Refrigerate and when it just begins to set, quickly fold in breadcrumbs; turn into serving dish or 1½ pint mould. Refrigerate for 2–3 hours. Sauce: cook damsons with sugar and water until soft, then sieve. Serve separately or, if using a mould, turn out and pour sauce over.

Baked York Ham with Spicy Raisin Sauce

Gammon weighing 4–6 lbs.   1 bay leaf   6 black peppercorns

GLAZE
1 tablespoon French mustard   1 oz. demerara sugar

SPICY RAISIN SAUCE
8 oz. granulated sugar   ¼ pint water   1 oz. butter   4 oz. seedless raisins
1 tablespoon Worcestershire sauce   4 tablespoons cider vinegar
Pinch each of ground nutmeg, mace and cinnamon   4 oz. redcurrant jelly

Total cooking time for meat 20 minutes per pound plus 20 minutes over. To ensure a succulent joint boil for half the time and roast for remainder. Place in large pan and cover with cold water. Bring to boil and throw away water to reduce likelihood of a salty joint. Cover again with cold water and add bay leaf and peppercorns. Bring to boil, cover, and simmer for half cooking time. Drain liquid and when cool enough remove the rind and score fat. Spread with mustard and sprinkle with sugar. Bake in pre-heated oven 400°F or Mark 6 for remainder of cooking time. Prepare sauce by dissolving sugar in the water and boiling for 10 minutes until slightly syrupy. Add remaining ingredients and simmer gently for 10 minutes until jelly has dissolved and raisins are plump. Serve hot with the ham.

Thirty-Nine

Sly Cakes

Rich Shortcrust Pastry
8 oz. flour   2 oz. hard margarine   2 oz. lard   1 oz. caster sugar   1 egg, beaten

FILLING
6 oz. dates (or dried figs) chopped   2 oz. currants   2 oz. raisins   2 oz. chopped walnuts
2 oz. dark soft brown sugar   Grated rind half lemon   6 tablespoons water
1 tablespoon caster sugar

Prepare the filling by putting the dates or figs, currants, raisins, walnuts, brown sugar, lemon rind and water into a pan. Heat gently, stirring occasionally until the mixture is soft and the water has been absorbed. Cool. Prepare the pastry by the traditional rubbing-in method and chill in the refrigerator for 20–30 minutes. Set oven to 375°F or Mark 5. Divide the pastry in two and roll out half to line a shallow 9 inch x 4 inch tin or one of equivalent area. Spread the filling evenly over the pastry and damp the edges with water. Roll out the remaining pastry and use to cover the fruit filling. Seal the edges well and bake in the oven for approximately 30 minutes until golden. Remove from the oven and sprinkle with caster sugar. Cool in the tin and cut into squares when cold.

Entrance to Valley Gardens, Harrogate

Homemade Lemonade

3 lemons   **2 tablespoons honey**
3 oz. caster sugar   **1½ pints boiling water**

Wash the lemons and remove the zest only, with a potato peeler or small, sharp knife. Put the zest, sugar and honey into a large heatproof bowl. Pour the boiling water over and stir to dissolve the sugar. Cover and leave until cold. Strain the liquid into a large jug and add the juice from the lemons. Serve chilled.

This bears no resemblance to the fizzy variety of lemonade available in the shops today. It is a delicious, refreshing drink well worth the minimal effort involved.

Carrot and Leek Soup

**1 oz. butter   1 lb. leeks, trimmed, sliced and washed   1 lb. carrots, peeled and sliced
1 medium potato, peeled and chopped   ½ level teaspoon curry powder
2 pints chicken stock   Salt and pepper**

Melt the butter in a large saucepan and add the vegetables. Cover and cook very gently for 10 minutes without browning. Add the curry powder and cook for 2 minutes, stirring, and then add the stock. Bring to the boil, reduce the heat and simmer for 30 minutes until the vegetables are tender. Cool slightly and pureé in a sieve or food processor. Season to taste and reheat to serve.

Cheese and Onion Oat Flan

PASTRY

4 oz. flour   4 oz. medium oatmeal   1 level teaspoon salt
2 oz. lard   2 oz. hard margarine   Cold water to mix

FILLING

2 medium onions, skinned and diced   2 spring onions, washed and sliced
1 tablespoon oil   2 medium eggs   ¼ pint milk   6 oz. Wensleydale cheese, grated
Salt and pepper

Set oven to 375°F or Mark 5. To prepare the pastry, put the flour, oatmeal and salt into a large bowl. Add the lard and margarine and rub into the dry ingredients until the mixture resembles breadcrumbs. Add sufficient water to mix to a firm dough. Turn on to a floured surface and knead lightly until smooth. Chill while you prepare the filling. Sauté the onions in the oil until soft and transparent. Mix together the eggs and milk and stir in two thirds of the cheese. Season with salt and pepper. Roll out the pastry to line an 8 inch flan dish and put the onions in the base. Pour in the egg/milk mixture and top with the remaining cheese. Bake for 40 minutes until golden brown. Serve hot or cold.

The Shipway, Robin Hood's Bay

Rhubarb and Orange Crunchy Crumble

1 lb. rhubarb, washed, topped and tailed and cut into 1 inch lengths
2 oz. granulated sugar   1 tablespoon water   Juice of one orange

CRUMBLE TOPPING
4 oz. wholemeal flour   2 oz. muesli   3 oz. butter   2 oz. soft brown sugar
Grated rind of one orange

Set oven to 350°F or Mark 4. Place the rhubarb, granulated sugar and water into a large saucepan and simmer, uncovered, until the rhubarb is soft. Remove the rhubarb with a draining spoon and place in a deep ovenproof dish. Reduce the liquid in the saucepan until syrupy and then stir in the orange juice; pour over the rhubarb. For the topping rub the butter into the flour and stir in the muesli, brown sugar and orange rind. Distribute the crumble mix evenly over the rhubarb and cook in the oven for 30 minutes. Serve hot or cold with plenty of cream.

Lemon Tarts

LEMON CURD
Grated rind and juice of 3 lemons   3 oz. butter   12 oz. caster sugar   3 eggs, beaten

PASTRY
6 oz. flour   Pinch salt   3 oz. butter   1 level tablespoon caster sugar
1 egg yolk   Cold water

The lemon curd can be made well in advance; it keeps for a month if stored in a refrigerator. Put the lemon rind, juice, butter and sugar in a large bowl standing over a pan of simmering water. Stir until the sugar has dissolved. Pour some of the mixture onto the beaten eggs and then pour this back into the bowl. Stir continuously until the mixture thickens, but do not boil. Pour into small jars and cover. Heat oven to 400°F or Mark 6. Put the flour and salt into a bowl and rub in the butter until the mixture resembles breadcrumbs. Stir in the sugar and mix to a firm dough with the egg yolk and a little water. Roll the pastry on a floured surface and use to line a 12-hole bun tray. Fill each pastry case with about 1 teaspoon of the lemon curd and bake until the pastry is pale golden brown and crisp. Cool on a wire rack.

METRIC CONVERSIONS

The weights, measures and oven temperatures used in the preceding recipes can be easily converted to their metric equivalents. The conversions listed below are only approximate, having been rounded up or down as may be appropriate.

Weights

Avoirdupois	Metric
1 oz.	just under 30 grams
4 oz. (¼ lb.)	app. 115 grams
8 oz. (½ lb.)	app. 230 grams
1 lb.	454 grams

Liquid Measures

Imperial	Metric
1 tablespoon (liquid only)	20 millilitres
1 fl. oz.	app. 30 millilitres
1 gill (¼ pt.)	app. 145 millilitres
½ pt.	app. 285 millilitres
1 pt.	app. 570 millilitres
1 qt.	app. 1.140 litres

Oven Temperatures

	°Fahrenheit	Gas Mark	°Celsius
Slow	300	2	150
	325	3	170
Moderate	350	4	180
	375	5	190
	400	6	200
Hot	425	7	220
	450	8	230
	475	9	240

Flour as specified in these recipes refers to plain flour unless otherwise described.